Freshwater Fish
Trout

Leo Statts

abdopublishing.com

Published by Abdo Zoom, a division of ABDO, PO Box 398166, Minneapolis, Minnesota 55439. Copyright © 2019 by Abdo Consulting Group, Inc. International copyrights reserved in all countries. No part of this book may be reproduced in any form without written permission from the publisher. Launch!™ is a trademark and logo of Abdo Zoom.

Printed in the United States of America, North Mankato, Minnesota.

052018
092018

THIS BOOK CONTAINS RECYCLED MATERIALS

Photo Credits: Alamy, Engbretson Underwater Photography, iStock, Shutterstock

Production Contributors: Kenny Abdo, Jennie Forsberg, Grace Hansen, John Hansen

Design Contributors: Dorothy Toth, Neil Klinepier

Library of Congress Control Number: 2017917512

Publisher's Cataloging-in-Publication Data

Names: Statts, Leo, author.

Title: Trout / by Leo Statts.

Description: Minneapolis, Minnesota : Abdo Zoom, 2019. | Series: Freshwater fish | Includes online resources and index.

Identifiers: ISBN 9781532122927 (lib.bdg.) | ISBN 9781532123900 (ebook) | ISBN 9781532124396 (Read-to-me ebook)

Subjects: LCSH: Trout--Juvenile literature. | Freshwater fishes--Juvenile literature. | Trout--Behavior--Juvenile literature. | Fishes--Juvenile literature.

Classification: DDC 597.092--dc23

Table of Contents

Trout..4

Body..6

Habitat...10

Food...14

Life Cycle...18

Quick Stats......................................20

Glossary...22

Online Resources............................23

Index..24

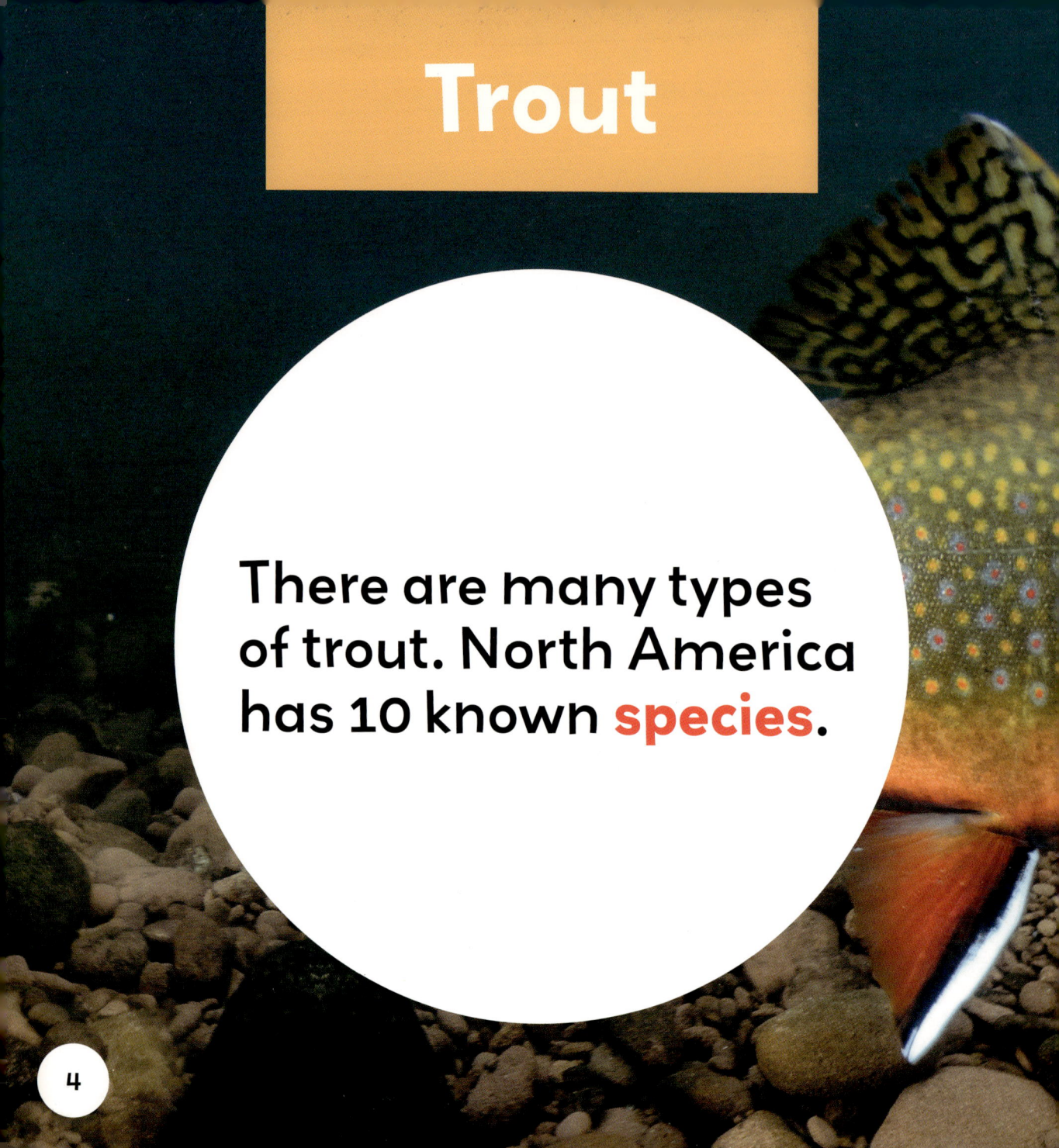

Trout

There are many types of trout. North America has 10 known **species**.

Trout are known for their excellent eyesight.

Body

Trout are covered in dark spots and tiny **scales**.

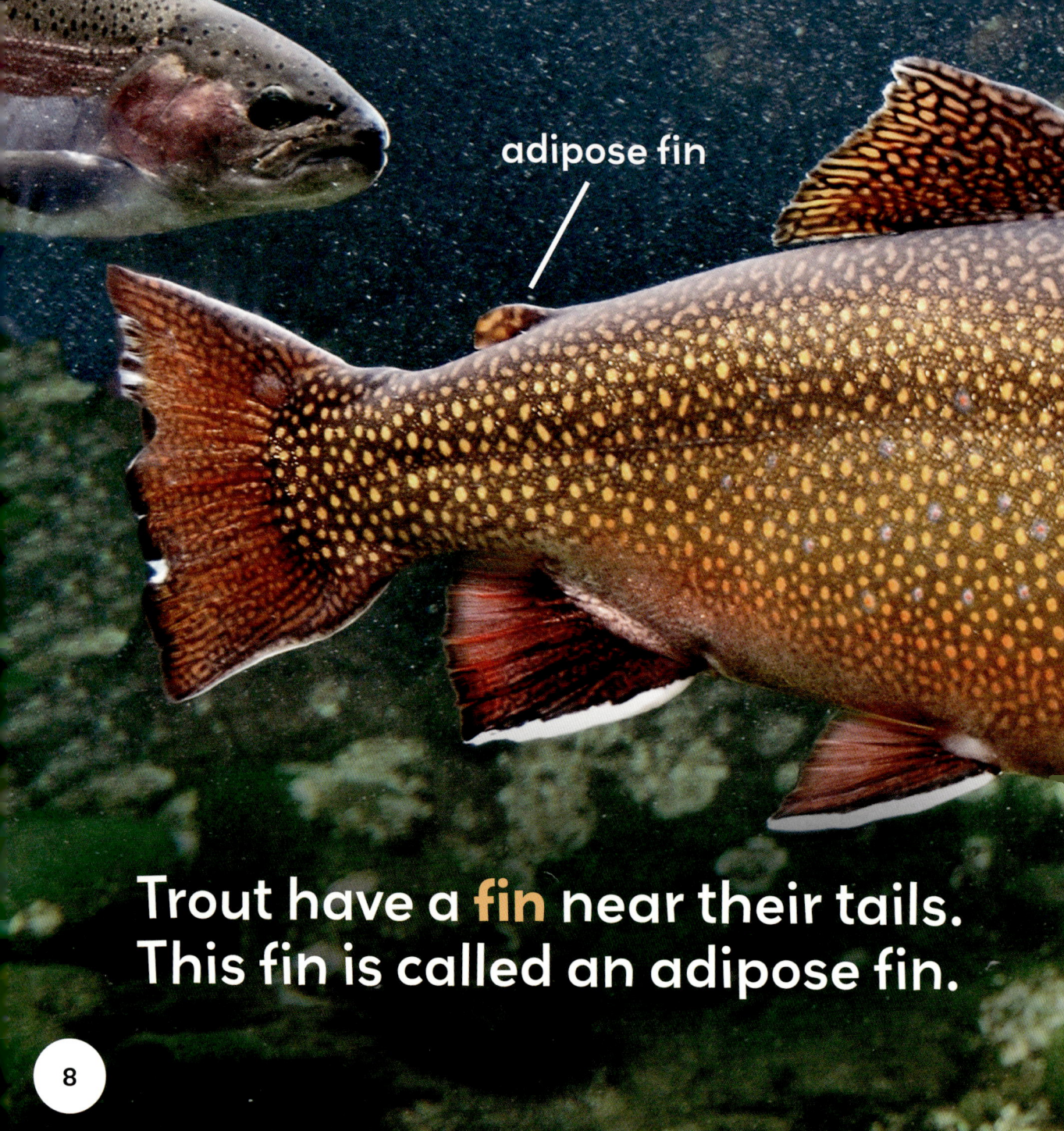

adipose fin

Trout have a **fin** near their tails. This fin is called an adipose fin.

Habitat

Some **species** of trout live in oceans.

But most trout live in cool, **fresh water**.

Many trout live in lakes. Some live in **streams** and rivers.

Food

Trout are **carnivores**.

They eat insects, fish eggs, and small fish.

Some eat small **crustaceans**. Young trout eat mostly **plankton**.

Life Cycle

Trout live an average of 7 years.

Female trout dig holes at the bottom of oceans, lakes, and **streams**. They lay their eggs there.

Average Weight

A rainbow trout is heavier than a textbook.

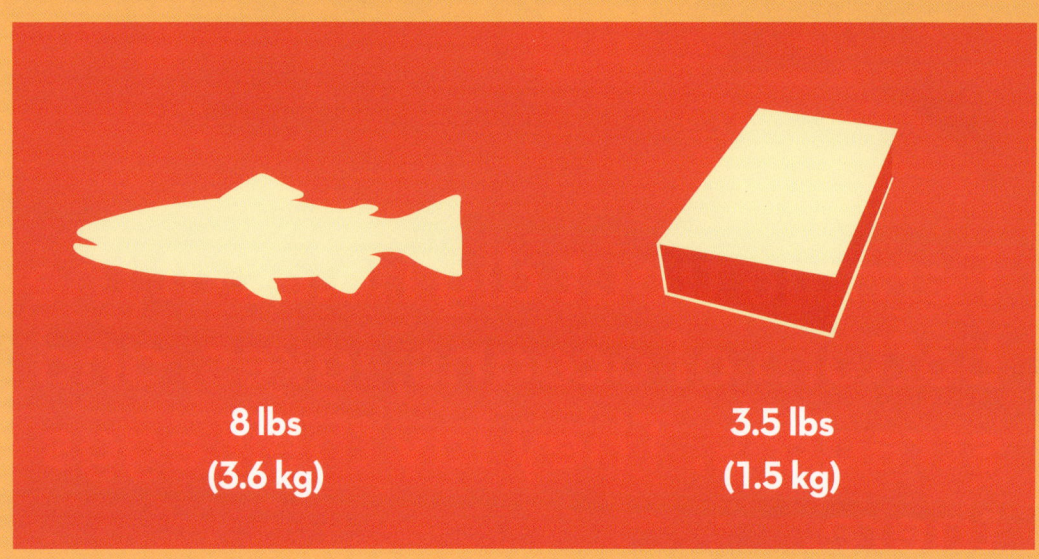

8 lbs (3.6 kg)

3.5 lbs (1.5 kg)

Average Length

A trout is longer than a basketball.

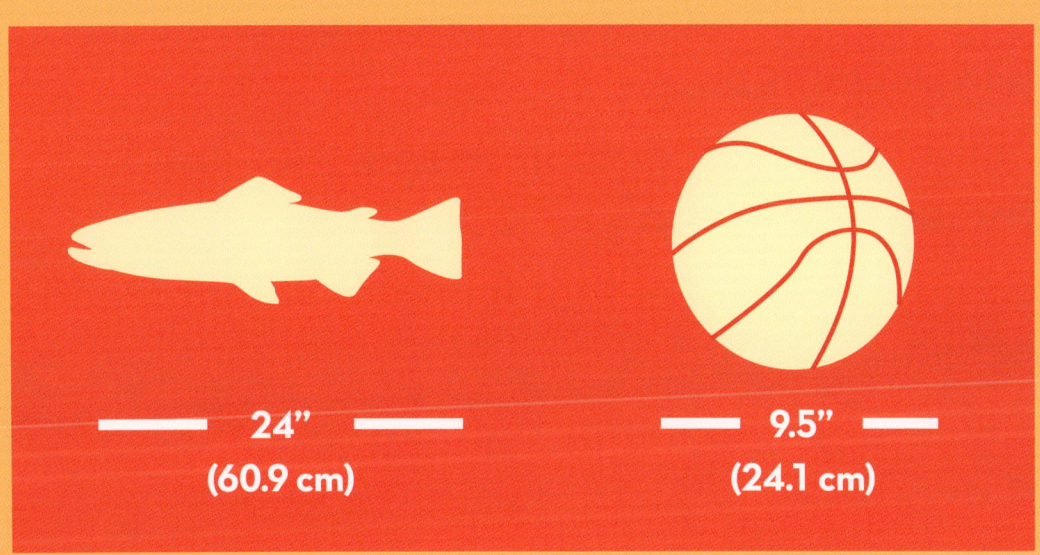

24" (60.9 cm)

9.5" (24.1 cm)

Glossary

carnivore – an animal that eats meat.

crustacean – a type of animal (such as a crab) that has many pairs of legs, and a body made up of sections covered in a hard shell.

fin – a body part of a water animal that is shaped like a blade or fan.

fresh water – water that does not have salt in it like oceans do.

plankton – a very small animal that drifts through the ocean.

scales – flat plates that form the outer covering of fish.

species – living things that are very much alike.

stream – a small, flowing body of water.

Online Resources

For more information on trout, please visit **abdobooklinks.com**

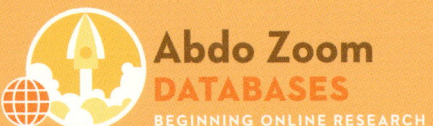

Learn even more with the Abdo Zoom Animals database. Visit **abdozoom.com** today!

Index

eggs 19

eyesight 5

fin 8

food 14, 15, 17

fresh water 12, 13, 19

habitat 11, 12, 13

lifespan 18

North America 4

salt water 11, 19

skin 6

species 4

tail 8